My Street

by Tom Gato
Illustrated by John Wallace

PEARSON

Glenview, Illinois • Boston, Massachusetts • Chandler, Arizona
Upper Saddle River, New Jersey

street

My name is Tom.
This is my street.

Look at my street.
What is new?

garden

Now it is summer.
What is new?
A garden is growing!

Now it is fall.
What is new?
I have new friends.

Now it is winter.
What is new?
It is cold.

playground

Now it is spring.
What is new?
We have a new playground.

Now it is summer.
We can see new things.